Think Like an Immigrant™

Old Lessons for Success Taught by
America's Newest Arrivals

Robert Wolff

Published by The Creative Syndicate

Think Like an Immigrant™

Old Lessons for Success Taught by America's Newest Arrivals

Robert Wolff

Published by The Creative Syndicate
10400 Overland Road, Suite 143
Boise, Idaho, USA 83709

Copyediting by Lynette Smith
Book Interior Design by Betty Abrantes

Book Information: www.RobertWolff.com

Print edition ISBN: 978-1-937939-04-5
Electronic edition ISBN: 978-1-937939-05-2
First printing 2011
Library of Congress Control Number 2011961674

PREFACE

Are you ready to change your life and get the things you want, but you don't know how?

That's all about to change if you follow the Immigrant's Principles for Success.

It's the 14 ways to greater success and prosperity.

What you're about to read isn't long, but the ideas it contains have the power to change your life.

They are the success principles immigrants follow. And if you follow these same principles and add to them the talents and abilities you already possess, you too can achieve remarkable results.

I was born and raised in a family of immigrants. As an adult, I have traveled to many parts of the world and spent time talking with and interviewing numerous famous immigrant celebrities and many others. In all these experiences, I've observed *14 Key Principles* immigrants live by, that are the foundation for their rapid and often spectacular success.

To *your* great success!

"...Give me your tired, your poor,

Your huddled masses yearning to breathe free,

The wretched refuse of your teeming shore.

Send these, the homeless, tempest-tossed to me,

I lift my lamp beside the golden door."

—Emma Lazarus,
from her 19th century sonnet,
The New Colossus

CONTENTS

Several years ago I visited Shanghai, China.

One Saturday evening, two friends and I went to see the Chinese Acrobats at a famous old Shanghai theater. After the show, my friends decided to take the 45-minute taxi ride back to the hotel.

I took the Rickshaw.

The time must have been around ten o'clock.

The air was crisp and the sky was beautifully clear, with a full moon that illuminated the city streets.

My driver—make that peddler, since the Rickshaw was a bicycle that pulled an attached carriage that could seat two— was a thin older man whose eyes lit up and whose smile flashed wide across his weathered face when he found out he was about to get such a good fare for such a long distance; ten US dollars for two hours of pedaling!

As we began our ride along the streets of downtown Shanghai, very quickly we were surrounded by hundreds of Chinese in their weekend threads riding bicycles. Men in suits, women in dresses, and children on bikes, all staring at the strange man in the back seat of the Rickshaw.

While the language heard all around me was impossible to understand, suddenly a young man pulled up to my left side and began speaking in words unlike any that were coming from the sea of humanity around me.

"Where are you from?" he asked.

Over all the noise, I yelled back, "America!"

"America! America! It is where I dream of going," he answered, with a big smile.

"Have you ever visited my country?" I asked.

"No," he replied. "But I have a map of America on my bedroom wall, and every night before I go to sleep, I look at that map and dream… dream of one day… that I will be in America."

"What kind of work do you do?" I asked, as we were being surrounded by more and more Chinese bicyclists who were now listening to our English conversation.

"Engineer… I am an engineer!" he shouted, "It is the dream of my life to see your country, meet your people and… live like an American."

Seeing his face and feeling the sincerity of his words and how they were spoken touched my heart.

We looked each other in the eyes and with all the inspiration I could find, I said to him, "Then you must come to my country. You must never give up your dream!"

As he dodged the other bicycles that were now making a somewhat frenzied attempt to get a closer look at the Saturday Night Rickshaw Show on the streets of Shanghai, my new fast friend came closer.

I reached out my hand for him to grab so I could pull him closer to the Rickshaw.

As we locked arms and he balanced his bike, he looked at me with tears now streaming down his face and soaking the lapel of his suit, and he said, "I don't know how I can come to America. I don't know when. I don't want my dream to die."

Seeing his face and hearing the sincerity of his words touched me deep inside.

Call it God, the Universe or whatever you wish, but it brought us two together on that Shanghai Saturday night—there are no accidents in this life of ours—for a moment so rare it could never be repeated.

As I pulled his arm and body closer to me, I leaned over at him and yelled over the crowd noise, "You will come to America and your dream will come true. Don't you forget this. Never give up, my friend. You hear me... Never!"

Tears were now pouring from his face, as he kept one hand on his handlebars and bent his head forward to wipe his tear-stained face on his sleeve.

He then raised his head and came closer to me and took his hand off of steering his bicycle and reached over in front of him to put his hand out to shake mine.

As we locked eyes and shook hands, these last words came from his lips:

"I shall never forget you and this night. And I will never give up my dream. Thank you. Oh, thank you!"

And with those words, we let go.

Suddenly, like a moment in time that stood still, he slowed down, ceased his pedaling and stopped in the middle of the street, staring at me as my Rickshaw pedaled away.

As I looked back at him being engulfed in the street by the swarms of bicycles and people, he continued to stare at me, waving goodbye until my Rickshaw turned down another street. As I turned the corner, with one last gaze toward one another over the crowd, we waved goodbye.

I have never forgotten my Chinese friend and that night.

It fills my heart with comfort to know—if he's like the millions of immigrants who have come before and will surely come after him—his will be a story of hope, inspiration and courage and will be a life filled with stories and lessons that can inspire us.

The Power and Influence of the Immigrant Is Everywhere— This Is a Country Built by Them

The English philosopher and commentator, G. K. Chesterton, visited America in 1921 and a year later published a famous assessment of the country's immigrant experience.

He noted that the U.S. had been engaged in an experiment... "the experiment of a democracy of diverse races which has been compared to a melting-pot... But even that metaphor implies that the pot itself is of a certain shape and a certain substance; a pretty solid substance. The melting pot must not melt." (*What I Saw in America,* 1922)

To Chesterton, then, it had shown no signs of melting. Its original form, which could be traced back to the nation's founding, was still firm.

It still is today.

We've never lost what makes this country so great. America is a noble land filled with goodness and people who care, but to many, the idea of everything good and noble that America stands for has been severely tarnished abroad.

The seemingly non-stop wars and many of our foreign policies have caused those from around the world to look upon this land and its people with disdain.

Yet, if history is our teacher, and at a time when so many Americans are wondering if we have lost our way as a country, we need look no further for the lesson and the answers than in the faces and lives of our people.

Us.

Immigrants all.

In all the history of this land, never has there been a decade without hardship, struggle, or a testing of our mettle.

The 1930s and the Great Depression.

The '40s and World War II.

The '50s and the Korean War.

Vietnam, race riots and the end of innocence in the '60s.

And so it goes.

But through every twist and turn in the road and all the celebrations and adversities, we, as immigrants, and we who have come from immigrants, have always risen to the challenge and have become a better nation and a people for the experience.

And along the way, we have learned many lessons.

Some on our own. Others taught by our parents, grandparents and friends who carried with them priceless stories and knowledge filled with the power to help anyone, simply for the price of a moment of listening.

As Americans we are all immigrants, and this is the strength of our nation. In celebrating our heritage and diversity, we can learn from the people who went before us, to help us to achieve our goals for the future.

It is to you, to them, and to my Chinese friend and untold millions like them, I write the words that celebrate the life, legacy, inspiration and wisdom of the immigrant.

How to Change Your Life and Get the Things You Want— The 14 Ways Immigrants Do It Every Day

Think Like an Immigrant is about to show you how to achieve greater success and prosperity in your life by using the Immigrant's Principles of Success.

America is a nation of immigrants. Legion are the rags-to-riches stories of immigrants coming to the United States—even without their knowing anyone or being able to speak English—and achieving great success in amazingly short times.

Think of it.

These are people from different lands. They don't speak the language and don't know the depth and mores of American culture. Many have decided to come here, knowing they may never return home. How is it that, under such adversity, fear and hardship, having to understand so much in so little time, they rise to such heights of achievement and success so quickly?

It happens every day.

And why is it that so many people who were born and raised in America's great land, with every potential for opportunity that the world has ever known, still complain about all the hardships and lack of opportunities available to anyone?

Immigrants—America's newest arrivals—can teach us why, and in ways we may have forgotten or may never have known.

These amazing people quickly reach the heights of success, not only for their quality and character, but for their work ethic and principles.

America is still the place immigrants dream of and will die for, just so they can live the dream and be called "An American."

What they're about to teach you can change your life.

And it all starts with Lesson 1…

LESSON 1

Use Time Wisely

Immigrants use *the compression of time*.

This means doing more but in the same amount of time.

They use the "Five Minutes to an Expert" solution of spending at least a few minutes each day on focused study of the subject(s) they wish to learn and excel at. And in the span of a month, those five extra minutes a day, spent learning whatever it is they want to learn, brings a huge increase of knowledge.

Immigrants also use *time deconstruction*.

By breaking down the things they do into small, easily achievable, quickly measurable parts for the achievement of their big dream, no matter how big the dream may be, that dream becomes more easily believable and achievable.

LESSON 2

Plan Carefully

Immigrants are careful and meticulous planners.

They see the road to reach their dream, long before they reach the destination.

They plan how and what to study.

They plan how and what amount to save.

They plan every part of their lives they have control over—just as an architect designs a home and a builder follows the blueprints—to construct it precisely the way they want their life to be.

There's no guessing or hoping things and events might happen.

The immigrant's call is one of "Action, Action, and More Action," for the immigrant knows that it is only by careful planning followed by action that they'll reach their goals.

LESSON 3

Spend and Save Sagely

The speed at which immigrants save money and buy their own businesses is amazing, and it's due in large part to the principle of "whole family saving" and "working toward a common goal."

The lesson is simple: No frivolous spending; you buy what you need.

And you buy what brings the biggest value for the investment.

Especially big-ticket items likes homes and automobiles.

Immigrants buy used cars that are well known for dependability.

They rent houses and apartments or buy only the least amount of home that will meet their needs.

Immigrants save the majority of the money they and the family make, and they invest it in safe investment vehicles so they won't lose the money they've worked so hard accumulating towards their ultimate goal.

Everything (but family) is sacrificed, if need be, for the attainment of the goal, and little is gambled or wasted to ensure its completion.

LESSON 4

Follow Worldly Success Principles

Immigrants know that the United States is the easiest country for anyone to succeed in, if they follow the 8 Principles of Success:

1. Dream a big dream.
2. Make a detailed plan on how to reach the dream.
3. Become knowledgeable in everything that will support and help them reach the dream.
4. Apply specific knowledge through daily focused actions.
5. Adjust plans whenever and wherever needed, based on new knowledge and understanding gained.
6. Always let go and get rid of the things, beliefs and ideas that are slowing down or preventing them from reaching their dream.
7. Hone their dream plan and actions so the two are perfectly in sync, until the dream is achieved.
8. Enjoy reaching the dream as they begin planning the next one.

LESSON 5

Stay on Dream, Don't Let Go and Adjust Where Needed

Giving up or quitting is not an option to an immigrant.

It's almost as if they have been hard wired and programmed to succeed, and nowhere in their psyche can they, or will they, accept the message to quit.

Immigrants are constantly adjusting their plans—*but rarely the goal*—based on the daily feedback they receive.

They are not attached to "how" they'll get there; they just know they will.

The result is always of greater importance than the ways they'll travel to reach the result.

Immigrants understand that while they may not be the fastest or savviest when they begin life in this country, they know that by the continuation of effort and daily action—even if it's only a small movement of action each day—it will take them to their goal, wherever and whatever it may be.

LESSON 6

Seek Wise Counsel

Being surrounded by family and friends they trust is highly important to an immigrant.

They know there'll be times—perhaps many times—when they will face tremendous adversity and roadblocks, getting from where they are to where they dream to be.

Immigrants are aware they won't always be understood.

They'll have disadvantages of being in a strange land with strange customs, cultures and rules they must live by. Yet having family and friends to talk to and share experiences and make common goals with, softens the adversity and gives the immigrant a new surge of power and strength and understanding—a constant renewal and daily recharge.

It's the safe soil that allows their dream to blossom and eventually to be harvested.

This sounding board of family and friends is vital, for it keeps the potentially harmful pride and ego in check, reinforces and builds self-esteem, and is a constant reminder to stay the course and not the let the winds of doubt, from being immersed in a new society and land, blow their ship of dreams onto the rocks.

LESSON 7

Live by the Formula:
Right Thinking + Right Action = BIG Results

Immigrants think differently.

They seek out those who are their mentors, inspirers and modelers, and they quickly study the steps and actions those great achievers took to become successful.

Then they copy those actions to achieve similar results.

Once immigrants arrive at their goal, they compare their service and business to that of the competition.

They continually hone and refine they way they do things, as well as implement different services and ways of doing business, to ensure their edge over others.

LESSON 8

Listen to Your Inner Knowing

One of the most admired and sought-after qualities an immigrant possesses is the innate ability to *listen to their gut feeling*.

The wise unerring counselor from within.

While we all have it, the immigrant "listens" to it and then acts on the messages, leadings and inspirations it gives.

This allows the immigrant to live anywhere and be a tremendous success, for this ability transcends countries and cultures, language or customs.

They *know* if what they're doing is the right thing to do, and they also *know* if it's the right way to do it.

Always.

LESSON 9

Make Fear and Desire Your Twin Friends

I mmigrants live by the two most powerful motivators of human action: fear and desire.

And they are masters of being motivated by both at the same time.

They are powerfully moved by the fear of not being successful and returning to conditions they sought so long to change.

On the other side of the coin, they have an unbendable will and desire to live the life they have imagined, fought for, cried for and would even die for.

How many of us can say the same?

Most people who have always known or have for too long lived the easy life, might choose just one of these as their prime motivator at any given time in their life.

Rarely both.

However, when the two are combined in ways the immigrant uses them, it's like pouring gasoline on a well-directed fire, as it becomes the propelling force for the attainment of the immigrant's dreams.

LESSON 10

Always Keep a Frame of Reference

A long with being deeply influenced and direct-
ed by fear and desire, immigrants also know the
kind of conditions they left in order to get into
this country.

The memory of what they left behind, and the
constant comparison of the two, propels them to
reach the dreams of their new life even faster.

Knowing what you've tried so hard and waited so
long to release from your life, can become an amazingly powerful motivator and guide that will keep you
on the right track—even when doubt comes knock-
ing on your door, often late at night or times when
you welcome it least.

One of the lessons immigrants can teach any of us is
that such hardship and adversity forces us to "wise up,"
to get rid of the chatter—the clutter and distractions in
our life—and to let go of the illusions and unworkable
beliefs about the way things have always been done.

Much too often, we fail to treasure the rare times
we are afforded in which to allow ourselves to be still
and listen.

Times when we can be illumined to the possibili-
ties of our lives and that "aha" moment that the dream

road you choose can be any road you wish, and the only force stopping you from walking down it is you.

Immigrants have the uncanny ability to focus on the right thoughts and do the right things to avoid hardship and pain.

Just think how much happier and wiser we could be if we did the same.

LESSON 11

Become a Master of Refinement

Immigrants are always open to criticism, as well as feedback.

In fact, they welcome it.

For such information gives them the perspective of looking at their lives and actions from the lens of those outside their lives, and it can often provide priceless knowledge and understanding they may not otherwise be able to see.

They look for and welcome new ways of doing the things they do and then doing them better.

They let go of the things that hold them back and embrace the new things that can help propel them more quickly to their goal.

And they keep honing and refining their learning and actions until their lives are so streamlined and effective that maximum results are achieved in less time and with less effort.

LESSON 12

Create a Burning Desire to Provide

While the immigrant may not understand the deep psychological roots for the why's of it, the three basic emotional needs of any human (beyond food, clothing and shelter) are:

- To be wanted
- To be needed
- To be appreciated

Think about it.

Woman or man, young or old, rich or poor, the need and desire to receive these three things is so great that stories are legion as to the lengths people will go and the actions they will take to receive them.

For the immigrant, being able to take care of and provide for their immediate family who may be here with them is important.

Yet what propels them even faster to their goal and dream is being able to help those less fortunate. And in many immigrants' lives, that means providing for friends and family who are still living in the land they left behind.

The immigrant knows how long it took them to reach the promised shores of America.

And once they arrive here, the weeks and months pass like days; and with each new day that passes, the sands in the hourglass of time trickle without end and with those sands, so does the time to provide for those less fortunate in their lives who can't or won't have their same opportunity.

The immigrant's desire to provide is incredibly time sensitive and unlike that of most people you may ever meet.

LESSON 13

Become Knowledge Hungry

Once immigrants arrived in this land, many had to take jobs (often holding multiple jobs at the same time) to support their families.

At the same time, many of them picked subjects they had an interest in and studied in the morning (before breakfast and work), during work breaks, lunch (which they packed themselves to save money and time so they could study), on the way to their other jobs (listening to MP3s and CDs in the car so they could learn English or any subject of their interest) and at night before bedtime.

Many immigrants have become experts in their chosen fields of vocation or interest very quickly.

The speed at which they attain specialized knowledge is astounding.

And it all goes back to the old principle that a few extra minutes of study each day turns any man or woman into an expert in a very short time.

LESSON 14

Develop a Laser-Like Focus and Purpose

I f, over the course of a day, you looked at what immigrants do and what they think, you would see that a *definiteness of purpose* is what drives their actions.

Unlike most people, who have no idea what they want, much less how and when they will achieve it, immigrants can tell you *exactly* what they want and what *specific* steps they are doing each day to achieve it.

Immigrants write down their goals, the costs, and the plans.

They study the advantages and disadvantages of achieving such a dream.

They break their goals down into many small pieces.

Their plan is so beautifully constructed that feedback is immediate and each small success is measurable, realizable and definable, and it becomes an inspiring springboard to the next dream and goal they desire.

Think Like an Immigrant
To Create the New Life You Dream

Inside you is the ability to create and live any dream, just the way you imagine it.

And it doesn't have to be completely different from anything that's ever come before it in order for it to be enjoyable or successful.

It just needs you to first give it life.

So begin using the Immigrant's Principles for Success.

But get ready.

Great things can happen when you begin to **Think Like an Immigrant**.

Share Your Favorite
Immigrant Success Story
with the World

If you have an immigrant success story about you, your family or friends, or you have a favorite story you may have heard, please send it to us and we might choose it to be in our next book.

Go to www.RobertWolff.com and click on the **Tell Me Your Story** tab for all the details.

Thank You and Best Wishes!

www.ingramcontent.com/pod-product-compliance
Lightning Source LLC
Chambersburg PA
CBHW030009040426
42337CB00012BA/713